Reach Out
Being Compassionate

Reach Out!

Learning to overcome negative thoughts and stay mindful is not the same as fighting depression. Do you feel overwhelmed by sadness? Remember, you matter. You are not alone. If you need help, reach out. Talk to an adult you love and trust. This could be a teacher, school counselor, or family member. Make an appointment with your doctor. Seek professional help. Or call the National Suicide Prevention Lifeline at 1-800-273-8255. Someone is available to talk with you 24 hours a day, every day.

45TH PARALLEL PRESS

Published in the United States of America by Cherry Lake Publishing
Ann Arbor, Michigan
www.cherrylakepublishing.com

Reading Adviser: Marla Conn, MS, Ed., Literacy specialist, Read-Ability, Inc.
Book Designer: Melinda Millward

Photo Credits: © Ljupco/istockphoto.com, back cover, 28; © RobMattingley/istockphoto.com, cover, 5; © CkyBe/Shutterstock.com, 6; © ANURAK PONGPATIMET/Shutterstock.com, 7; © Syda Productions/Shutterstock.com, 8; © Puckung/Shutterstock.com, 10, 14, 26; © SDI Productions/istockphoto.com, 11; © vovk 12/Shutterstock.com, 12; © Motortion Films/Shutterstock.com, 15; © Samo Trebizan/Shutterstock.com, 16; © Monkey Business Images/Shutterstock.com, 17; © feelplus/Shutterstock.com, 18; © wavebreakmedia/Shutterstock.com, 19; © photka/Shutterstock.com, 20; © veronchick_84/Shutterstock.com, 22; © Odua Images/Shutterstock.com, 23; © freesoulproduction/Shutterstock.com, 24; © Sergey Novikov/Shutterstock.com, 27; © MidoSemsem/Shutterstock.com, 28; © Wavebreakmedia/istockphoto.com, 29; © Vitalina Rybakova/Shutterstock.com, 30

Graphic Element Credits: © kkoman/Shutterstock.com, back cover, front cover, multiple interior pages; © str33t cat/Shutterstock.com, front cover, multiple interior pages; © NotionPic/Shutterstock.com, multiple interior pages; © CARACOLLA/Shutterstock.com, multiple interior pages; © VikiVector/Shutterstock.com, multiple interior pages

45th Parallel Press is an imprint of Cherry Lake Publishing.

Library of Congress Cataloging-in-Publication Data has been filed and is available at catalog.loc.gov

Printed in the United States of America
Corporate Graphics

Table of Contents

INtRoDuCtioN

Have you ever seen someone in pain? Have you ever seen someone cry? We don't like to see others **suffer**. Suffer means to feel pain. Often, we feel sorry for those who suffer. We want to make things better.

Compassion is a sense of shared suffering. It inspires people to help. Compassionate people show kindness. They understand that all humans suffer. They try to understand the feelings of others. They take actions to help. They want to ease the pain.

This book gives you tips on how to be **mindful**. Mindful means being aware. It means taking care of your body and mind. Take a moment. Practice being compassionate. Just breathe …

Tip: Choose to be compassionate.

CHAPTER ONE
Suffer and Heal Together

It's important to be mindful of other people's suffering. Listen to what they say and how they say it. Pay attention to their body movements. Find out what they need. Sometimes it's helpful to use your own suffering to help others. Think about how you'd want someone to treat you when you're sad.

Think of a hard time in your life. Recall what happened. Recall how you felt. Try to feel the pain.
- Say, "This is a moment of suffering. I feel …"
- Say, "Suffering is a part of life. I am not alone."
- Say, "I must be kind to myself. I must be kind to others."

· · · · · · · · · ·➤ **Tip**: Keep a journal. Write about things that caused you pain.
Then, write about how you can make yourself feel better.

Prepare yourself to be a good friend. Be open to listening. Sometimes, showing compassion means being a good listener. Get yourself in the right mood to listen.

- Breathe in. Breathe out. Do this several times.
- Close your eyes.
- Think of a color that you connect to compassion. The color should feel warm.
- Imagine the color all around you.
- Imagine the color entering your chest.
- Imagine it going to your heart.
- Imagine it slowly spreading throughout your body.

When you need to be compassionate, recall this color. Imagine the color flowing through your body. Imagine the color spreading to your friend. Remember how loved and supported you are. Direct the love and support to your friend.

Tip: Hug yourself. Hug others. (But remember to ask permission first.)

Real-Life Scenarios

Life is full of adventures. There will be challenges. Things happen. Make good choices. These are some events you could face:

- You see someone being a bully. You have a choice. You can say something. Or you can do nothing. What do you do? Explain your thinking.

- You learn that your friend's grandmother died. You see your friend crying. How does this make you feel? What can you do to make your friend feel better?

- You and your friend tried out for the soccer team. You made it. But your friend didn't. Your friend tells you it's okay. But you know your friend is upset. What do you do? How can you be kind to your friend?

CHAPTER TWO
Be a Good Friend to Yourself

Good friends are important. Take care of your friends. They will take care of you. But it's also important to take care of yourself. When you take care of yourself, you will be better able to take care of others.

Sometimes, we can be our own worst judge. Learn to be a better friend to yourself.

- Recall a time when a friend felt bad. How did you help your friend? How did you talk to your friend?
- Recall a time when you felt bad. How did you talk to yourself?
- Think about the differences. Why would you treat yourself differently?
- Practice talking to yourself in a kind way. Practice being your own best friend.

• • • • • • • • ➤ **Tip:** Gently put your hand over your heart. Feel the pressure and warmth of your hand. Feel the beat of your heart.

Try this writing activity:

- Think about what you don't like about yourself. Write about how this makes you feel.
- Pretend you have the most compassionate best friend in the world. This friend knows you very well. This friend loves and accepts you, no matter what.
- Pretend you're the best friend. Write a letter from this person's view. Show compassion. Show understanding. Show support.
- Read this letter every time you feel anxious or bad about something.

Before you can be a good friend to others, you need to be a good friend to yourself.

Tip: Make friendship bracelets. Hand them out to your friends. This reminds them that they are not alone.

Science Connection

Having compassion is good for the body. It can reduce the risk of heart disease. It makes people feel happy. It boosts the positive effects of the vagus nerve. Dr. Stephen W. Porges is a brain scientist. He calls the vagus nerve the "compassion nerve." He found this nerve is connected to caretaking. It is connected to compassionate behaviors. The vagus nerve is a bundle of nerves. It starts at the top of the spinal cord. When someone sees suffering, the vagus nerve is sparked into action. It sends messages to other body parts. It can create a warm feeling. Our bodies like this feeling. So we are more likely to do good deeds. We want to keep the positive feelings.

CHAPTER THREE
Turn an Enemy into a Friend

It's easy to be compassionate to a friend. But what about an **enemy**? An enemy is someone you don't like. An enemy is someone you constantly disagree with. Remember, everyone deserves kindness. Enemies are humans too. Being compassionate means being nice to your enemies as well.

Try to understand others. This includes your enemies. Be mindful of what others are going through.

- Imagine this person's history. What was this person like as a child? Who is this person's family? Where does this person live?
- Imagine this person's day or week. Is this person going through a bad time? What bad things have happened to this person?

Kid Pick!

tle: _____

uthor: _____

icked by: _____

_____

/hy I love this book:

_____
_____
_____
_____
_____
_____
_____

lease return this form to
Mrs Heather in Youth Services or email
our review to
gunnell@rockfordpubliclibrary.org

 ROCKFORD PUBLIC LIBRARY

········► **Tip:** Don't react too quickly, especially in anger. Pause. Take a deep breath in. Let it out.

When people are mean, it's usually not about you. It's about them. They may be going through something. Try to be understanding. Believe that people are good. Reach out. Show compassion by taking the first step.

Turn enemies into friends. Here are a few ways to do this:

- Say sorry. Admit to being part of the problem. Share how you can improve.
- Focus on the good things. **Compliment** them. Compliment means to say good things. Do this to their face. Do this behind their back.
- Find a connection. Talk about something you have in common.
- Find something they're good at. Ask for help. Ask for advice.

Tip: Leave nobody behind. Make sure that you invite people to events. Don't leave anyone out.

CHAPTER FOUR
Sign Up to Volunteer

Volunteers are people who freely offer to do something. They aren't paid. They want to help people and communities. They make a difference. They're happy people. They're compassionate.

Here are some tips for volunteering:

- Believe in your power to do good.
- Learn all you can about the people or organization you're helping.
- Show up early. Stay the whole time. People count on you. So, do what you say you will do.
- Journal about your experience. This will help you remember the impact you had on others.
- Be friends with other volunteers. Work together!

18

Tip: Keep track of when others have showed compassion toward you. Write it down.

Here are some ideas for volunteering:

- Go to a public place. Examples are beaches and parks. Pick up **Litter**. Litter is trash. But be safe! Make sure to use gloves. Don't pick up anything that's sharp.
- Go to an animal **shelter**. Shelters are places for unwanted animals to stay. Spend time with the animals. Pet them. Clean their cages. Help them get adopted.
- Visit a senior citizen's community. Talk to the people who live there. Play games with them. Offer to be a pen pal. Be their friend.
- Go to a **food bank**. These places give food to people who need it.

Tip: Help people in your neighborhood. Get to know your neighbors.

Spotlight Biography

Mother Teresa was born in 1910. She devoted her life to caring for the sick and poor. She's famous for her compassion. She was born in Macedonia. She taught in India for 17 years. She was a nun. Nuns are women who belong to a religious community. She founded the Order of the Missionaries of Charities. This is a women's group. In 1979, she got a Nobel Peace Prize. She died on September 5, 1997. In honor of Mother Teresa, the United Nations made her death date the International Day of Charity in 2013. A few years later, in 2016, she was declared a saint. She was named Saint Teresa of Calcutta. Calcutta is the capital of India. Mother Teresa said, "Never worry about numbers. Help one person at a time and always start with the person nearest you."

☮ CHAPTER FIVE
Forgive Others

Holding on to **grudges** is unhealthy. Grudges are bad feelings. You hold on to grudges when you can't get over what someone has done to you. These **negative** feelings can cause a lot of worry and heartache. Negative means bad. To **forgive** means to let go. It means to stop feeling mad at someone for doing something wrong. Forgiveness is a high level of compassion. The act of forgiving is good for everyone. It makes everyone feel better.

First, make a list. Is there anyone you need to forgive? Think about why you're angry. Write down how you feel. Write down why you feel that way.

• • • • • • • • ➤ **Tip**: Make a list of all your feelings. It's okay to be mad. But remember, feelings can change.

Second, manage your anger. Find ways to stop being mad. Cry. Don't try to hold back tears. It's okay to cry. Go outside. Yell as loudly as you can. Think of it as releasing your negative feelings. Exercise. Go on a walk. Be active. Sometimes this helps us feel better. Talk to a trusted adult or a professional. Third, forgive everyone on your list. Take your time. Decide who and when you want to forgive. Forgiving someone is very hard to do. But it can be done.

Remember, we all make mistakes. We're human. Understand why people act the way they do. Write the person a letter. Or talk to the person. Or forgive the person in your mind. Keep it simple. Set new rules for your relationship. Forgiveness does not mean forgetting. If someone has hurt you multiple times, it's okay to stop being that person's friend. But this doesn't mean you have to stop being friendly.

· · · · · · ·▶ **Tip**: Pretend you're in a maze. Take your time walking out of it. Know that you will eventually get out.

Fun Fact

Louisville is a city in Kentucky. It's called the Compassionate City. It has a world record for the most volunteers and acts of compassion. It has had this record since 2013. In 2017, the city had over 180,000 volunteers and acts of compassion. Every year, it hosts a program called Give a Day Week of Service. Citizens do community service during this week. Volunteers have built beds for homeless people. They have sent goods to refugees in other countries. They have hosted clean-up events. This program was started by Mayor Greg Fischer in 2011. Fischer said, "The beauty of this annual Week of Service is that it puts a spotlight on the compassion that we know happens in this community every single day, though we might not always see it. Every year, I learn about new things that people are doing throughout this community to help build each other up. And it's amazing."

CHAPTER SIX
Do an Act of Kindness

Acts of kindness are when people do nice things. Compassionate people try to be kind all the time. It's hard work. It's not easy fighting against negative feelings.

Compassion must be practiced. Try to do nice things as much as you can. Do it because you know you'll make other people happy. Do it because it'll make you happy. Start small. Small acts of kindness make a big difference.

Here are some examples:

- Walk your neighbor's dog for free.
- Write your teacher a "just because" thank-you note.
- Make dinner for your family.
- Do chores you don't normally do.

········> **Tip**: Think of kindness as a river. Rivers flow over sharp rocks. They keep moving. They make rocks smooth.

It's easy to do kind things for your loved ones. Have you tried to do something nice for someone you don't know? Try to do a **random** act of kindness for a **stranger**. Random means unplanned. Strangers are people you don't know.

Here are some examples:

- Let someone go in front of you in line.
- Compliment a stranger.
- Open doors for other people.
- Smile at someone you pass in the hallway.
- Give up your seat on the bus.
- Help carry someone's bag.
- Take a picture for someone.

Your act of kindness will most likely be "paid forward." This means if you're kind, other people will be kind. Spread compassion everywhere!

Tip: Remember to be smart and safe when interacting with strangers.

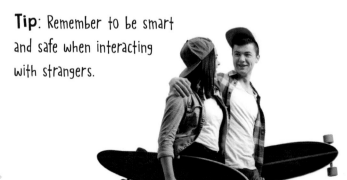

HOST YOUR OWN MINDFULNESS EVENT!

Hearing too much bad news in the world? Do you and your friends want to be more kind? Do you want to be more loving? This might be the best time to host your own mindfulness event! Help find some inner peace. Host a "Be Compassionate" Party!

STEP ONE: Figure out where you can host your party. You'll need space to spread out.

STEP TWO: Make invitations—and get creative! Ask a friend to help you. Send out the invitations.

STEP THREE: Plan your activities and get supplies.

Appreciation Box!

- Get a box with a lid. Cut a slot in the lid. Slot means opening. Decorate it.

- Ask everyone to write messages of appreciation on pieces of paper. These can be thank-you notes. These can be positive messages.

- Put the messages inside the box.

- Sit in a circle. Pass the box around and take turns reading the messages.

- Talk about each message. Ask, "How does this message make you feel?" and "What did you learn about yourself?"

- Encourage people to keep putting messages in the box.

Write Around!

- Sit in a circle.

- Give each person a piece of paper. Have each person write their name on the top.

- Pass the paper to the right. Each person needs to write a kind comment about the person named on the paper.

- Set a timer for 3 to 5 minutes. Pass the paper to the right when time's up.

- Repeat until everyone has written a kind comment on every paper.

- Have each person read the comments to themselves.

- After everyone has read their comments, ask them to think about these questions:

    - How are you a kind person? How can you be more kind?

    - Who is the kindest person you know? What makes that person the kindest?

Community Care Circle!

- Choose a "talking piece." This is an object. It means only the person holding it can talk.

- Ask, "How are you feeling right now?" Pass the talking piece around. Let each person share.

- Ask, "When was the last time you showed compassion? What did you do?" Pass the talking piece around. Let each person share.

- Ask, "When was the last time you needed compassion? What did you need? What can we do for you?" Pass the talking piece around. Let each person share.

GLOSSARY

compassion (kuhm-PASH-uhn) sense of shared suffering that inspires people to be kind and helpful in order to ease the pain of others

compliment (KAHM-pluh-muhnt) to praise, to say good things

enemy (EN-uh-mee) not a friend

food bank (FOOD BANGK) a place that collects and stores food to give to people in need

forgive (fur-GIV) to pardon or release someone from wrongdoing

grudges (GRUHJ-iz) bad feelings of resentment brought on when someone wrongs you

litter (LIT-ur) trash

mindful (MINDE-ful) focusing one's awareness on the present moment to center the mind, body, and soul

negative (NEG-uh-tiv) bad

random (RAN-duhm) unplanned

shelter (SHEL-tur) a place where an unwanted animal can stay

stranger (STRAYN-jur) someone you don't know

suffer (SUHF-ur) to feel pain

volunteers (vah-lun-TEERZ) people who freely offer to do something

INDEX

ABOUT the AUTHOR

Dr. Virginia Loh-Hagan is an author, university professor, and former classroom teacher. She recently volunteered at a food bank in Montreal, Canada. She lives in San Diego with her very tall husband and very naughty dogs. To learn more about her, visit www.virginialoh.com.